Robert Kirkwood

Illustrated by Edward McLachlan

 LONGMAN

To Mandy, Adam, Vicki, Philip, Jonathan, Anna, Fiorenza and Rula

Contents

Introduction

This book is first of all an attempt to give secondary school pupils a simple taste of the philosophy of religion. It is somewhat bare of the sorts of religious facts that are generally to be found in textbooks for its aim is primarily to move away from the 'information orientation' of religious studies to an exploration of religious ideas.

It is secondly an attempt to deal in a simple and direct manner with the conceptual confusions and questions that many children have about God. My own experience is that these confusions are numerous and that there is therefore little point in saturating children's minds with factual details of different religious traditions when the concepts they have with which to interpret these details are so muddled.

One disastrous lesson from my early days in teaching illustrates the point. The subject of the lesson was Buddhist symbolism. I focused especially on the symbols associated with the Buddha himself and talked at length about such things as the long ear lobes, the third eye, the different postures and the small lump to be found on the top of the Buddha's head. I also of course explained that these were all thought to be symbols of the Buddha's divinity and spiritual wisdom. The lesson seemed to have gone well. The pupils appeared to have a genuine interest in the topic and in a subsequent test they were nearly all able to recall the main symbols talked about in the lesson. Any sense of self-satisfaction I had completely evaporated, however, when during a later discussion lesson one pupil raised his hand and said: 'Sir, my brother's got a dirty great big lump on the side of his nose . . . Does that mean he's a Buddha?' The question unfortunately was genuine and what was more distressing was the fact that many others in the class also thought the question was perfectly fair and sensible. I had to spend a good deal of time trying to explain that there was no relationship whatsoever between acne, warts and moles and spiritual wisdom.

The problem of course was that my lesson had avoided any study of the central religious concepts involved (i.e. divinity and spiritual wisdom) because it was based on the assumption underpinning many religious studies books and courses, that children are able to make the jump unaided from the factual details about religion to the spiritual dimension that gives meaning to the facts. My own experience is that most children can make no such jump and that many are prevented from doing so by a confused understanding of the concepts central to the study of religion (e.g. God, spirit). *Looking for God*, then, attempts to facilitate this jump by addressing itself directly to some of these confusions.

The book is thirdly an attempt to meet some of the needs of mixed-ability teaching; it tries to provide material that will appeal to children right across the ability range. Each chapter thus begins with work simple and I hope stimulating enough to be attempted by children of all abilities, including the virtual non-reader. Each chapter then increases in difficulty with the aim of stretching the more able child in the class.

The book is finally intended to encourage the greater use of philosophy of religion in the classroom with children of all abilities. My own personal experience of this approach has been encouraging. It has not only provided me with a more direct route to tackling the problems and questions that children have about religion but it has also managed to generate in many of them a renewed interest in religious studies.

Robert Kirkwood

1 Should the girl 'give up', or should she look somewhere else? Give her some advice.

2 Most people, when they were very young, had some sort of idea of where God lives. Think back to your own early ideas and draw a picture to illustrate them.

GOD IN THE SKY

Lots of people still **talk** as if God lives somewhere **UP** in the sky.

Lots of people still **act** as if God is somewhere **UP THERE**. People praying, for example, will often bow their heads in respect as if God were **above** them.

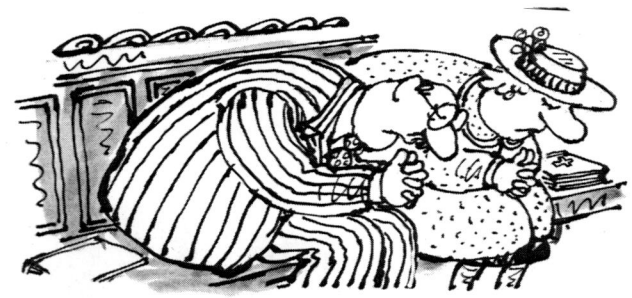

Sports players often do the opposite. When they make a mess of things, they will often look UPWARDS and say a few angry words, as if they are talking to God in the sky . . .

1 Make your own list of things people say and do which give the impression that God lives **UP** in the sky.

2 Think about where *you* would start to look for God and then write your ideas down in a poem entitled 'Looking for God'.

A WRONG UNDERSTANDING OF THE UNIVERSE

People who expect to find God living in the sky are usually said to have a **pre-scientific** understanding of the universe.

They think that the universe is something like a three-storey house, with **God** on **top**, **men and women** in the **middle** and the **Devil** in the **basement**.

The universe is not like this.

The sky is not a roof, the earth is not a floor and there is no fiery devil living beneath our feet.

If God exists then and we are to have any hope of finding him, we must give up this childish view of the universe, otherwise we shall waste our time looking in the wrong places.

DON'T FORGET – the earth is round so it doesn't really make sense to talk about God being somewhere 'UP' there.

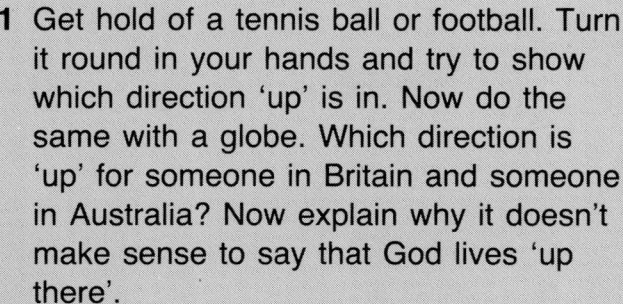

1 Get hold of a tennis ball or football. Turn it round in your hands and try to show which direction 'up' is in. Now do the same with a globe. Which direction is 'up' for someone in Britain and someone in Australia? Now explain why it doesn't make sense to say that God lives 'up there'.

2 Make a list of possible reasons why many people believe that God lives above our heads and the Devil beneath our feet.

3 **Library work**
In the second century AD, a man called Ptolemy put forward his new theory about the structure of the universe. Find out what his theory was. Now look up information about Copernicus, who was a sixteenth-century astronomer. Find out what his theory about the structure of the universe was. Compare the two theories and illustrate your written answers with carefully drawn pictures.

1 Most people, when they were younger, had some sort of picture of God in their head. Think back, and draw this picture on your own 'Missing Person' poster.

(NB: People whose beliefs prevent them from answering this question should move on to question 2.)

2 Why do you think that many people say that God is male? Give as many reasons as you can for your answer.

GOD AS SOME-BODY OR NO-BODY

If God has a body, he must be finding it difficult doing the sort of things God is supposed to do.

LIKE WHAT?

Well, if he created the universe – how did he do it with a body like ours?

And there must be millions of people who pray to God every day. How is he able to listen to them all if he only has two ears like us?

I'm getting the engaged tone..

He told me to hang on..

God is also supposed to know about everything that's going on in the universe. That must be a big problem for someone with only two eyes.

God is also believed to be everywhere at the same time. This would be very tiring for a God with a body like ours.

If God exists, and we are going to find him, we should perhaps stop looking for a being with a body like ours. God restricted to a body like ours would find it very difficult being God.

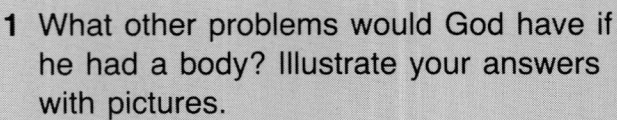

1 What other problems would God have if he had a body? Illustrate your answers with pictures.

2 Conduct a small survey among your family and friends. First of all, ask them what they think God looks like and write down their replies. Next, ask the ones who believe that God has a body to give their answers to the list of problems you worked out for question 1.

GOD -MADE IN OUR IMAGE

Now we seem to have a real problem, because if God doesn't have a body he can't be male *or* female. Various religious books, however, seem to encourage us to think of God in human terms. In the **KORAN** (Muslims), the **VEDAS** (Hindus) and the **TORAH** (Jews), God is always talked about as if 'he' were male. The **NEW TESTAMENT** (Christians) also gives this impression by referring to God as a **father** who cares deeply for his children.

Does this mean then that these religious books are completely wrong in their ideas about God?

WORDS AS PICTURES

Before answering this question, we should remember that words can be used as pictures. Look, for example, at what this girl is saying.

John's a right old **PIG!**

True.

Now, it's obvious that John doesn't have the body of a pig but that doesn't mean to say that the girl is wrong because she isn't trying to say that John looks like one. Instead she means that John's eating habits are best described or 'pictured' by the word pig.

In other words, John eats like a pig.

Many people believe that religious books are also using **words as pictures** when they use human terms to describe God. They are not thought to be saying that God has the body of a human man when they call him a king, lord or father. They are rather thought to be saying that using these words helps to paint a picture of God's **behaviour** to us. The word 'mother' might also be a helpful picture.

Perhaps then it is still useful to describe God in human terms if we see these words as helpful ways to understand God's **nature** rather than his **appearance**.

1 John doesn't have the body of a pig. Explain then why it would be unfair to say that the girl is lying when she calls John 'A right old pig'.

2 Why is it possible to use human terms like 'king' or 'father' to describe God even though he doesn't have a human body?

3 Many religious people have compared God to a man. What would *you* compare God to if you were trying to explain your own idea of God to someone else?

4 Read the following passages from the New Testament in the Bible and explain why Jesus thought that the word 'father' was a helpful picture of God.

Matthew chapter 6, verses 5–14, and verses 24–34
Matthew chapter 7, verses 7–12
Matthew chapter 10, verses 26–31

1 Are these people looking in the right places? Give reasons for your answer.

2 What do you think is meant when religious people say that 'God is a spirit'? Draw a picture to go with your answer.

GOD IS A SPIRIT

Many people think of ghosts when God is said to be a **spirit**, and ghosts for most people are usually greyish-white beings, with see-through bodies, who love creeping up on people and scaring the living daylights out of them.

When God is said to be a **spirit**, he is often thought to be a sort of good 'ghost' who prefers helping people to frightening them.

Giving God a see-through body, however, is the same as giving him a solid one. We are still giving him a **shape**, and by giving him a shape we are giving him all the problems we talked about in the last chapter.

When religious people say that God is a spirit, they are not trying to say that God is like a ghost. They are rather trying to say that God cannot be restricted by any sort of shape, solid or see-through, because if God is to do all the things God is supposed to do, he must be **shapeless** and so, of course, **invisible**.

Let me out! I've got to be EVERYWHERE!

---

1 What do you think a ghost might be? You could write a ghost story to illustrate your answer.

2 Explain in your own words why many religious people say that God cannot be a ghost.

3 Make a list of all the different ways the word 'spirit' can be used in sentences. For example: 'That girl's got spirit.' What does 'spirit' mean in this sentence? Write simple sentences to illustrate the different meanings of 'spirit' that you have found. Do the meanings have anything in common?

GOD IS A POWER

Trying to find a being that is **shapeless** and **invisible** is a problem but perhaps it becomes easier if we begin to think of God as a **FORCE** or **POWER** that expresses itself in the universe. Looking for God then becomes similar to looking for any other sort of power that we think might exist.

Well when, for example, you look for the POWER of ELECTRICITY, you don't recognise it by its **shape** but rather by what it **does**.

WHAT?

Need any help, Dad?

CLICK!

Do you mind!

The same is true when you look for the POWER of the WIND. You don't look for any kind of shape, but you *do* look for the sorts of things that you know that wind can do.

Don't disappear Wayne – Tea's ready.

If God is a POWER then, perhaps we should look for him in a similar way. We should not look for something with a recognisable shape. As with electricity or wind, we should be looking for evidence of how God's power expresses itself in the universe.

What sorts of things is this POWER supposed to do?

Religious people often say that God's power is unlike any other sort of power in the universe because it is **CREATIVE**, **THOUGHTFUL** and **LOVING**. Looking for God then becomes a question of searching our universe for possible expressions of God's CREATIVITY, THOUGHT and LOVE. If we find *them* then perhaps it's possible to say that we've found God.

1 Why might 'looking for God' be similar to looking for electricity or the wind?

2 What do religious people believe to be the difference between the power of God and any other power in the universe?

3 **Research work**
The following passages from the Bible give examples of people who claim to have been influenced by God's power. Read them carefully and then explain briefly what they are claiming in each case.

1 Samuel chapter 17, verses 12–51
John chapter 9, verses 1–41
John chapter 11, verses 1–44

Look at what everyone in this picture is saying. The girl thinks that the universe may have been made by God and the boys think that it may have been the result of an accident. What do you think? Give as many reasons as you can for your answer.

In the first book of the Bible (Genesis chapter 1) it says that the universe and everything in it was made by a **CREATIVE POWER** called **GOD** and that this power finished the first part of its work in **SIX DAYS**.

Books on science, however, seem to give a different story. They often say that the universe started off with a **BIG BANG** and that things as we know them today took many **MILLIONS OF YEARS** to **EVOLVE**.

Look at the picture above of a man standing between seven squares. These squares represent seven days. Draw a larger version of this picture. Now read Genesis chapter 1 and fill in the squares with pictures to show what Genesis says was created on each of the six days. What is the seventh square for?

This has led to all sorts of arguments between those who believe in the six-day Bible story of creation and those who believe in the scientific theory that the universe took millions of years to evolve.

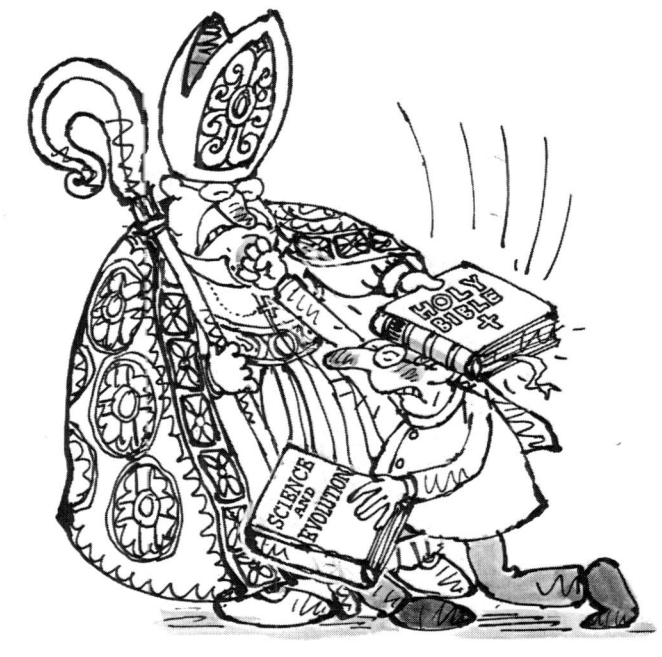

Many religious people, however, now say that these arguments are unnecessary, and that it is possible to believe in both versions.

Well, these people don't see this as a problem. They point out that this is just another example of the same truth being told but in different ways.

Well, look at these two children. They are both interested in finding out where they came from, so they are both asking the same questions.

It's clear, however, that they couldn't be given the same detailed answer because their minds are at different stages of development. One is only three years old and wouldn't be able to understand a scientific explanation. The other is 14 and wouldn't find this sort of explanation at all difficult.

So both would need to be given different versions of the same truth. The three-year-old would need to be given a simplified version, helped perhaps by using picture-language. The 14-year-old, however, would need to be given a more scientific account of THE FACTS OF LIFE. Both versions would of course tell the truth but each would tell the truth in different ways to suit different minds.

Here are two more people asking the same question.

Where did EVERYTHING come from?

These people couldn't be given the same answers, either, because their minds are also totally different. The man on the left lived 3000 years ago and couldn't possibly understand a scientific explanation. The twentieth-century woman on the right, however, would have few problems understanding this sort of answer.

Both then would need to be given different versions of the same truth because their minds are at different stages of development. The pre-scientific man would need a simplified version, helped perhaps by using picture-language, while the twentieth-century woman would need a more scientific account.

Many religious people believe that this is why **Genesis** and the **theory of evolution** say different things. Genesis is thought to be a simple picture-language answer to the same sort of questions that the theory of evolution tries to answer. Both versions then tell the same truth but they tell it in different ways, to answer the questions of different minds.

> Now we live in a scientific age can't we chuck Genesis away?

Well, many religious people say 'No'. They point out that another reason why Genesis and the theory of evolution seem to be saying different things is that – as well as answering the same questions in different ways – the main questions they are really trying to answer are totally different.

Genesis is said to be more interested in trying to answer the questions 'Who caused **the Big Bang**?' and 'WHO CAUSED ALL THE DIFFERENT FORMS OF LIFE TO APPEAR?' The scientific theory of evolution, however, is said to be more interested in answering questions like 'What happened after **the Big Bang**?' and 'HOW LONG DID IT ALL TAKE?'

Many religious people therefore believe that these two versions are not in competition with each other. They don't see any reason to chuck either of them away because both versions are believed to actually help each other out. Genesis is said to tell science that **the Big Bang**, the universe, life and evolution are no accident but rather the work of a CREATIVE POWER called GOD, while science is said to tell Genesis **how God worked after the Big Bang**.

BANG! See! I told you it wasn't me!

1 On page 21 it was said that Genesis and the theory of evolution are two ways of explaining the same truth. In your own words, explain why two versions were said to be necessary.

2 Give your own example of an occasion when the same question from two different people might have to be answered truthfully in different ways. Write a short play to show how you would answer each one.

3 In the text above it is said that Genesis and the scientific theory of evolution are trying to answer different questions. In your own words explain what these different questions are.

4 **Research work**
Charles Darwin wrote a book called *The Origin of Species* to support the theory of evolution. Find this book in the library, read the last page and try to work out whether or not he believed in God.

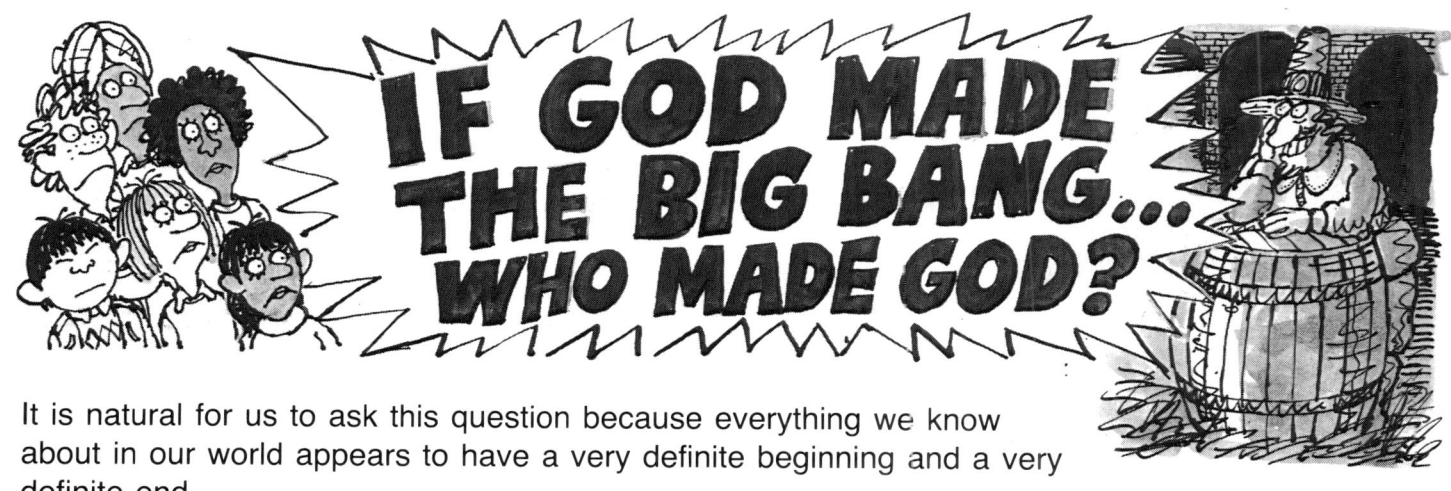

IF GOD MADE THE BIG BANG... WHO MADE GOD?

It is natural for us to ask this question because everything we know about in our world appears to have a very definite beginning and a very definite end.

Religious people, however, say that there is a **POWER** in our universe that has no beginning and no end. They say that this power is **ETERNAL** and **INFINITE**, and the word they use to describe it is **God**. So for religious people the question 'Who made God?' makes no sense because they point out that if God had been made by another power, he wouldn't be God, because 'God' is the word they use to describe the **eternal and infinite power** that is responsible for everything in the universe. Religious people then say that God must therefore be unmade because if God is to be God then he must have no beginning.

But why not just say the universe is ETERNAL?

Lots of people say exactly this. They get rid of the idea of God by saying that **MATTER** (or, in other words, the universe itself) is **INFINITE** and **ETERNAL** and is not the work of an infinite and eternal creator.

People must, of course, make up their own mind about this. They must decide for themselves whether it makes more sense to believe in an **eternal, infinite GOD** or in **eternal, infinite MATTER**. It is important, however, to understand one thing: either way involves **BELIEVING** in an idea that is beyond present human understanding, because either way brings you face to face with the whole mystery of **how anything can exist without first having a beginning**. Believing then is something that both religious and non-religious people do.

OUR idea of eternity is INFINITELY better than yours, so there!

ETERNAL GOD!
Eternal GOD!
ETERNAL MATTER!
ETERNAL MATTER!

1 Look back at page 23. Explain in your own words why religious people say that it makes no sense to ask 'Who made God?'

2 Explain what you understand by the words 'eternal' and 'infinite'. Use a dictionary to help you.

3 This chapter suggests that in order to explain the existence of the universe we must believe either in an **ETERNAL, INFINITE GOD** or in **ETERNAL, INFINITE MATTER**.
Explain which belief makes more sense to you. Perhaps you can think of an alternative to these two beliefs. If so, try to explain it simply in a short paragraph.

4 Look at the picture and model below. They are both trying to represent ideas of **eternity** and **infinity**. Explain how they do it?

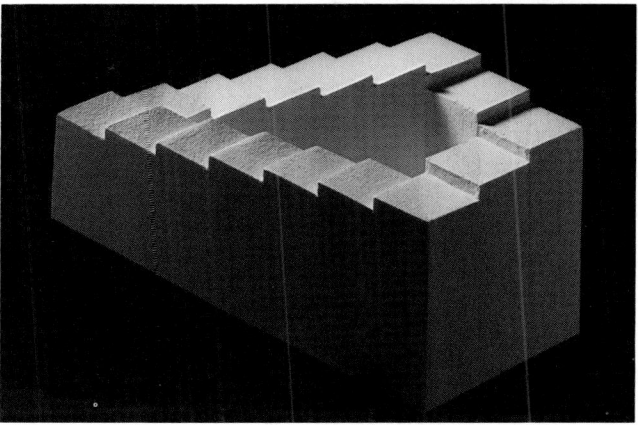

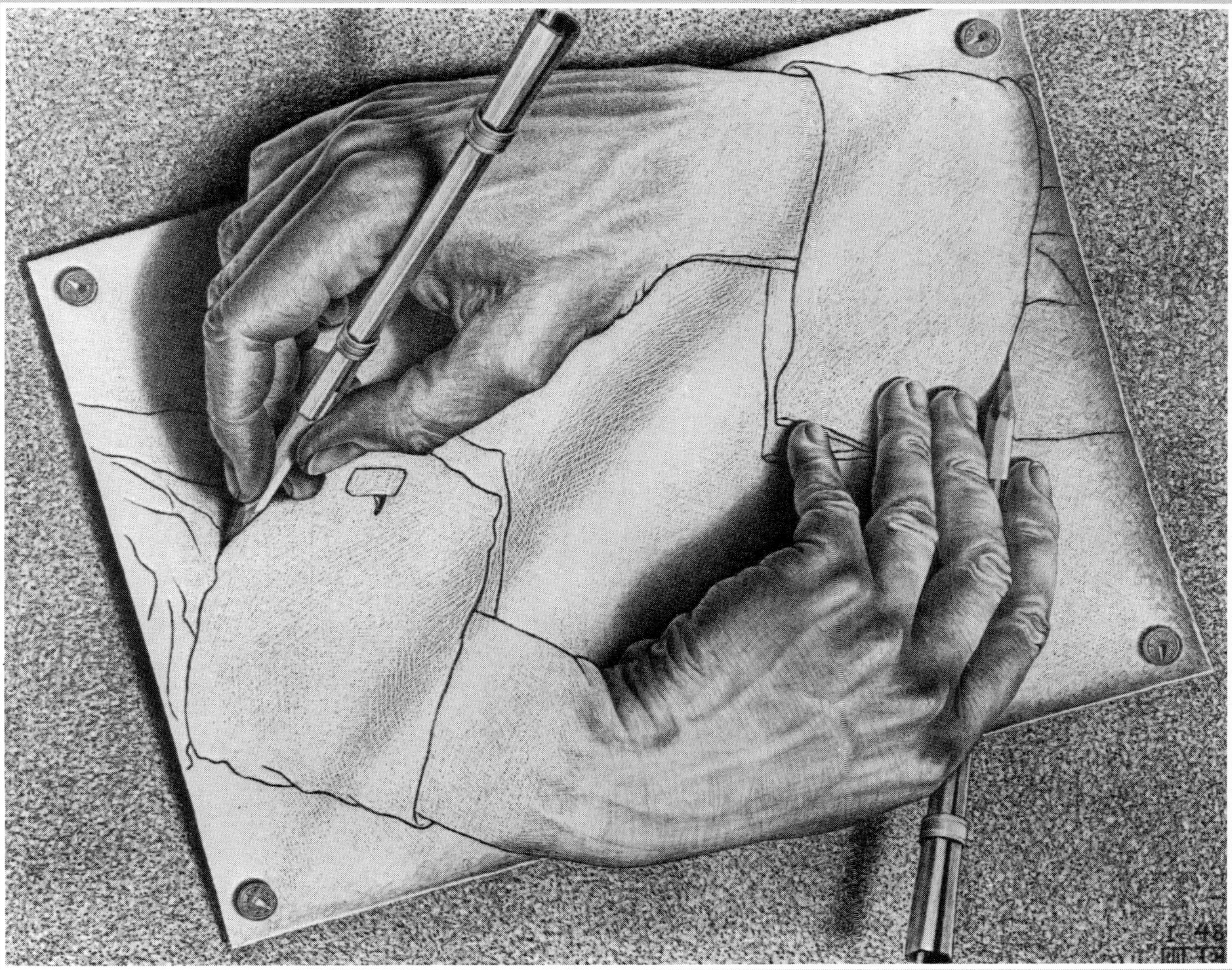

5 Read the story below. How does this give an idea of infinity?

A man sets out to walk one mile. First, he walks half a mile; then he walks half of the half a mile left; then he walks half of the remaining distance, then half the distance again, and so on, and so on . . . Whatever the distance left, he has to walk half of it first. He walks and walks and walks – but he never reaches the end of his journey.

(NB: This diagram will help you to understand the problem.)

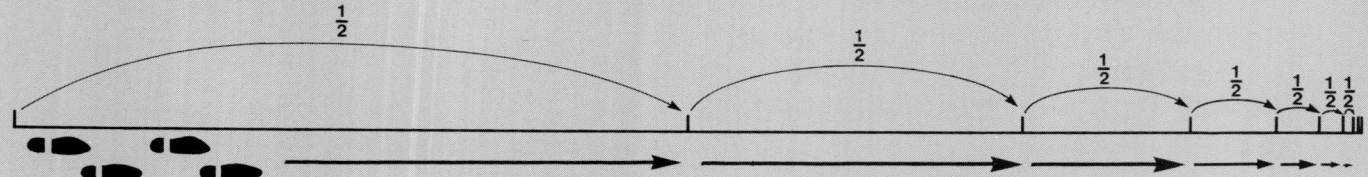

6 Follow the instructions to make the Möbius Strip. Explain why this could be said to be a good illustration of eternity and infinity.

Möbius Strip
Take a strip of paper, give it a half-twist and stick the ends together. Take a pencil and starting from any point on the strip draw a line along the middle of the paper. You will see that you never have to turn the paper over; it only has one side. Now take a pair of scissors and cut along the line you have drawn. The result will help you to answer the question above.

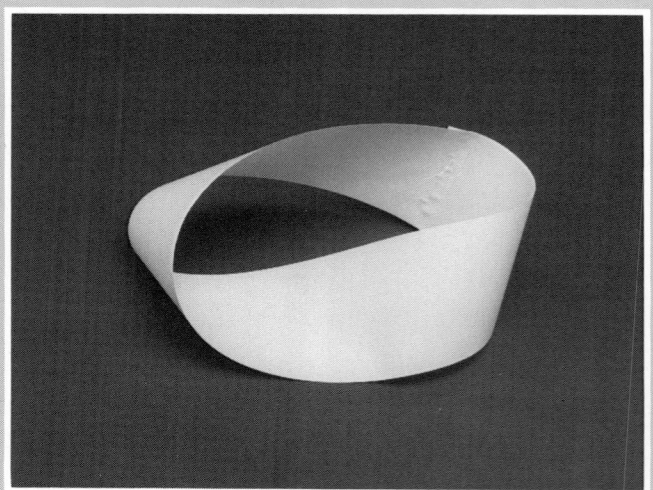

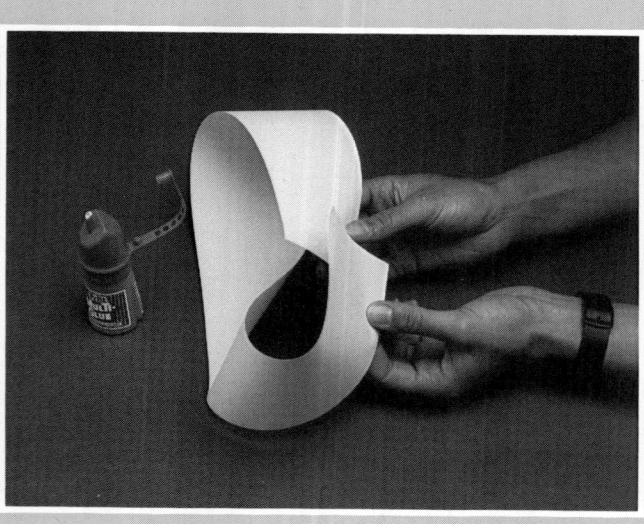

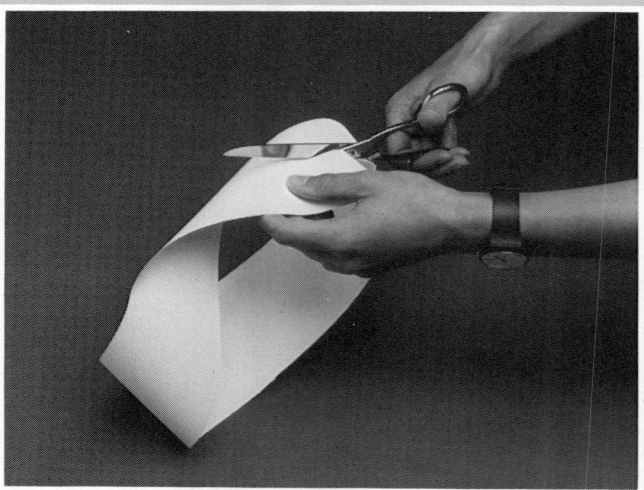

7 Now draw your own picture to represent eternity and infinity.

1 If God did make this world, what can we say about him from looking at the things he has **designed**?

2 Just suppose you could have designed the world? What changes would you have made?

GOD AS A DESIGNER

It is often said that one very good reason for believing in God is that so many things in our world seem to have such **complicated designs**.

The human brain, for example, is more complicated in design than any computer and can do many more things.

Animal and human eyes, ears and noses have a superior design to any similar human-made machine and they also work better.

And human arms and legs are also more efficiently designed for movement than anything we have yet managed to build.

Many religious people therefore believe that all of this design in our world must mean that there is a **DESIGNING POWER** responsible for it all. They call this power **GOD**.

To illustrate this point, think of a camera. No one coming across a camera for the first time would say that the different parts from which it was made had come together by chance. The **design** of the camera would force a person to believe that it had been designed and put together by an **intelligent, designing mind**. In this case, a camera-maker.

Well, I think there was this BIG bang and all these little pieces flew together and..... What is it?

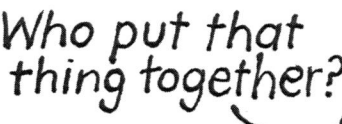

Who put that thing together?

... And this one, ladies and gentlemen, takes first prize!.... THE EYE!.... full colour, self focusing, automatic, lense cleaner, no flash needed.....

Many religious people therefore say that if this is true of a camera then no-one should say, for example, that the different parts of the human eye came about by chance. The design of the eye (which is far more complicated than a camera) should also force us to believe that it was put together by an **intelligent, designing mind**. Religious people call this mind **GOD**.

---

1 Religious people often try to give evidence for God's existence by talking, for example, about the design of cameras and the design of eyes. Explain what they say.

2 Can you think of anything wrong with this argument?

3 Read Psalm 19 in the Bible. Does the writer of this Psalm believe in a designing God? Give reasons for your answer.

IS GOD A CRUEL DESIGNER?

Many people point out that if God designed everything in the universe then he must be very **cruel**.

The world for example seems to have been made with an **in-built design** for earthquakes, volcanoes, hurricanes and things of that nature which can cause terrible pain and suffering.

They also point out that the design of this world allows millions of people to **suffer** and **die** each year of **poverty, disease** and **war**.

People who think like this often decide therefore that the power behind the universe is either cruel, uncaring or non-existent.

When you buy something from a shop, and it goes wrong, you can either take it back or write a letter of complaint. If you could write a letter of complaint to God, what complaints would you make about the world? (You might actually prefer to write a 'thank-you' letter or perhaps a bit of both.)

A POSSIBLE SOLUTION TO THE PROBLEM OF EVIL

To try to answer the charge that the evils in this world make belief in a caring God very difficult, it is important to start by dividing different forms of suffering into two types. First of all, there is the **suffering caused by human beings** and secondly, there is the **suffering caused by nature**. There are then two questions that religious people should try to answer:

Firstly, why did God create a creature who is capable of so much cruelty?

And secondly, why did God design a system of nature that can cause so much suffering?

WHY DID GOD DESIGN CRUEL CREATURES LIKE HUMAN BEINGS?

OUR MACHINE MAKER WHO ART IN HEAVEN SINCLAIR BE THY NAME GIVE US THIS DAY OUR DAILY DATA...

Most religious people will answer the first question by saying that God did not want to design **puppets** or **robots** that would always do what he wanted because they had no choice.

Instead, they say, God wanted a creature that would *choose* to do his will. God therefore designed this creature called a human being with the gift of **FREE WILL**, and so with the ability to act either lovingly or cruelly.

Religious people therefore believe that much of the suffering in this world is caused by human beings misusing God's gift of free will and by their choosing to act in a way that causes hunger, poverty, pollution, disease, wars and the suffering and death of innocent people. Suffering is seen then as a necessary risk that comes with designing people rather than robots.

1 Explain in your own words how a religious person would explain why God didn't want to design human beings like programmed robots.

2 If God had designed us as robots with no free will, do you think your life would have been better? Think about what robots are like; think about things like heat, cold, food, drink, feelings, friendships.

3 In the future, it may well be possible for human beings to make robots that can be programmed to behave like us in every way. If you had to make a choice, would you prefer to have this sort of robot as a friend, or a free-choosing human being? Explain your answer. (Perhaps you can write your answer by making a list of the advantages and disadvantages of being a robot.)

WHY DID GOD DESIGN A SYSTEM OF NATURE THAT CAUSES SO MUCH PAIN?

Religious people often answer this second question by saying that if we are to be creatures with free will and not automatic robots, then we've got to live in a world that allows us to make **real choices** between good and evil. If God then had made a world in which there was no sort of pain, we would have no real choices to make because anything we ever chose to say or do could never be harmful and so would always lead automatically to good.

You could therefore **choose** to throw yourself out of the classroom window during a boring lesson without any fear of injury at all.

Or you could choose to throw all sorts of things at your teacher because they would never do any damage. In fact, it would be the same as choosing not to throw them.

Caring then for yourself and others would not only be unnecessary but probably also unimaginable since there would be no real difference between caring and not caring.

Now it is clear that in order to make a world where no sort of pain exists possible, the **LAWS OF NATURE** could not be fixed. They would have to change constantly with every possibility of pain and death. For example, gravity would either sometimes work or sometimes not.

Or objects would sometimes be hard and sometimes soft.

And the laws which control the evolution of our world and which cause things like volcanoes and earthquakes would have to be postponed whenever there was someone around who could be hurt.

With these sorts of alterations, the study of science would of course be impossible. The laws of nature would change so often that they would never be stable and so they couldn't be investigated and understood.

Many religious people believe that if these sort of changes took place and the possibility of pain and suffering disappeared, then our **free will** would also disappear because there would be no real choices to make.

For example, choosing to be caring, kind, unselfish, sensitive and loving would be a waste of effort.

Because choosing to be the opposite wouldn't cause harm – and so wouldn't be wrong.

Many religious people would therefore say that our present world, with all its possibilities of pleasure and pain, is the only sort of world that God could have created for creatures that he wishes to freely **CHOOSE** him rather than **evil**.

1 Explain in your own words why many religious people believe that a world where pain and suffering are possible is the only sort of world that God could have made for creatures like us.

2 Do you agree with this argument? Give reasons for your answer.

3 **Research work**
Hindus believe that some of us suffer more than others because of what they call 'the law of karma'. Find out what you can about this law and write a short paragraph to explain its meaning.

4 Read John chapter 9, verses 1–7 from the Bible, and say whether you think Jesus believed in the law of karma. Give reasons for your answer.

1 Why do you think that prayers sometimes don't appear to get answered?

2 Most people, at some time in their life, have made requests to God. Try to think of an occasion when you did, and explain what happened.

GOD AS PERSONAL

When religious people say that God is **personal**, they usually mean that the **CREATIVE** and **DESIGNING POWER** responsible for the universe actually cares about us and our problems.

Many people, however, find this difficult to believe. They talk about personal requests that they have made to God and which haven't been answered.

These people therefore often come to the conclusion that God either doesn't care about us or just doesn't exist.

Such people, however, probably have a wrong understanding of God and **prayer**. Very often they seem to treat God like a Mafia godfather and prayer as an opportunity to extract favours. They tell him then what they want and when they don't get it they feel let down.

Thinking religious people, however, don't treat God or prayer like this. He is not seen as a power that guarantees them protection from all suffering, and prayer is not seen as some kind of 'perk' that goes with believing in him.

God is rather seen as an **ALL POWERFUL, ALL KNOWING** being who created and designed us and who therefore knows our needs better than we know them ourselves.

Religious people then would say that they are more interested in **GOD'S WISHES FOR THEM RATHER THAN THEIR WISHES FOR GOD**. They will, of course, make requests, but their main concern is to treat prayer as an opportunity to talk and listen to God and to find out his will for their lives, rather than as a chance to pull a few strings to get their own way.

1 When Jesus knew he was going to die, he went to a quiet and private place to pray. Read his prayer in Luke chapter 22, verses 39–45 and explain what it tells us about his attitude to God and prayer.

2 **Research work**
Muslims follow the religion of Islam. Find out what the word 'Islam' means and explain what this tells us about the Muslims' attitude to God and prayer.

KNOWING GOD'S WILL

Religious people therefore believe that we should all be trying to find out **God's will for our lives** rather than trying to impose our will on him. The problem then, however, is HOW TO DISCOVER WHAT IS GOD'S WILL AND WHAT ISN'T.

Don't worry — It's God's will!

I don't think it's God's will that I should die!

There doesn't seem to be an easy solution to this problem but many religious people say that part of the answer is to get to know God's **PERSONALITY** and that then we will begin to understand what sorts of things God wants from us and what sorts of things he could not possibly want.

WHAT ARE YOU TRYING TO SAY ?!?

Well, imagine coming home from school one day and finding a letter supposedly from your Mum saying:

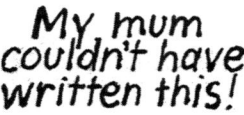

If you know something of your Mum's personality and you know, for example, that she is a very honest person, then you would of course become suspicious of the letter. You would probably think that what the letter says isn't in character with what you know of your Mum's personality. You would then no doubt decide that the letter could not possibly be from your Mum and that she would never want you to do this sort of thing.

In the same sort of way, if you know certain things about God's PERSONALITY then you will also become suspicious of believing that God would want you to do or ask for certain things rather than others.

This means that if we are to get to know God's will for our lives then, as with any other person we try to understand, we must seek to experience God's personality for ourselves.

1 If a rubber came flying across the classroom and hit you on the head, who would you begin to suspect? Make a list of your chief suspects and also a list of those who you think wouldn't have done it.

2 Now try to work out what made you put certain people into particular lists.

3 You probably put certain people into particular lists because of what you know about their **personalities**. Write a list of the many different ways in which we can get to know about each other.

4 If God exists, and if he's got a personality, how do you think we could get to know what it is like?

EXPERIENCING GOD'S PRESENCE

Religious people often say that their first **experience of God** comes to them as a strange **feeling** or **sense** that they are not actually alone in the world. They talk of an uncanny experience of being **watched** and of being in the **presence** of some being that is different from and more powerful than themselves and other human beings.

I DON'T GET IT!

Think back to those times when perhaps your mum and dad went out for the night and left you alone in the house. It's dark outside, of course, the television isn't working and you're sitting alone in the living room with only a comic or a book to read.

CREAK!

HORROR

Lots of people in that situation of course start to **feel** or **sense** that perhaps they are not actually alone in the house. They begin to feel that something is there with them, perhaps even watching them. They are not sure what it is but creaks on the stairs, noises in upstairs rooms and memories of horror films usually work on their imagination and convince them that it is either a burglar or even perhaps a ghost. This then usually leads to all sorts of feelings of fear.

Well, this experience of not feeling alone in the house, although not exactly the same and although usually just the work of an overactive imagination, can nevertheless help us to understand the experience of religious people.

They also, for example, are convinced that they are not alone but in the **presence** of something other than themselves.

They are also partly convinced of this by the things they **see** and **hear** around them.

43

And they also experience a sort of **fear** at the thought of being in its **presence**, although this is not a fear of danger but more a sense of **DREAD** or **AWE** at being in the presence of something greater than themselves.

Religious people are not, of course, talking about the presence of imaginary ghosts or burglars in houses but about the presence of God himself in the **world around** and **inside us**. They would also say that their experiences of his presence are not based on their insecurity or imagination but on an honest sense of life's wonder and mystery.

1 Religious people very often talk about experiencing God. Explain why some religious people say that this experience is similar to those we experience when we are alone in a house.

2 When we are alone in a house, squeaks on stairs and noises in upstairs rooms can help to convince us that we are not alone. What sort of things convince religious people that they are not alone in the world but always in the presence of God?

3 Special occasions can sometimes give people this experience of being in the presence of a power that is greater than themselves, for instance, staring at the stars at night or standing quietly in front of the sea. Have you ever had similar experiences? Give examples.

4 Read Psalm 23 in the Bible and explain what this writer thought the presence of God was like.

EXPERIENCING GOD'S WILL

The first friend might be said to have no **will power**. He or she doesn't offer you any sort of opposition. They agree with everything you say and are prepared to do whatever you do. Such people we often call **weak-willed**.

Religious people say that while the first part of experiencing God is **experiencing his presence**, the second part is **experiencing his will power**.

It may help to understand what they mean if you think, for example, of the difference between a friend who always agrees with everything you say and one who is prepared to argue with you.

The second friend, however, is not like this. He or she will always oppose you if they don't agree with what you're doing or saying. Such people are said to have **a will of their own**.

Religious people believe that God is like this second friend. He is also believed to have a **will of his own** and is said to be constantly **arguing** and **struggling** with us about what we are **doing, saying** and **becoming**.

I can't hear God's voice arguing with me!

Me neither!

Religious people say that this argument and struggle goes on in the silence of your own head and that the argument and struggle is usually between **what you want to do** and what God says **you ought to do**. The following Hindu poem illustrates what religious people mean.

But this struggle inside me is often unclear....so how can I be sure what God wants from me?

Methinks, by this time I have become mad; otherwise why should I feel so troubled inside every now and then? When I remain quiet with the undisturbed mind, I see that SOMEONE speaks loudly from within— "I AM HERE! HERE I AM!" In the dimness of the sky of my heart, methinks, I see Some One come to my side; He moves, He speaks, He plays, — He smiles, — He indulges in a hundred other sports!..... If I try to leave him off and live alone, I cannot; it seems He has settled His dwelling in the core of my heart!

Well, religious people believe that our understanding of this struggle and therefore of God's will can be made clearer by reading and studying certain **HOLY BOOKS**.

These books are believed by many of their readers to be God's **personal letters** to us. They are said to contain special stories and messages which seek to give us a deeper understanding of **God's will**. They tell us, for example, that we are all struggling and arguing with a **divine will** that is **holy, righteous and loving** and which is striving to **create and design** a world that is the same.

Religious people therefore believe that this sort of understanding of **God's will** can help us to understand his struggle with **OUR will**. It teaches us, they say, that the whole purpose of the struggle is to create and design in us a person who, like God himself, is **CREATIVE, THOUGHTFUL, PERSONAL, HOLY, RIGHTEOUS AND LOVING**.

1 Religious people often say that experiencing God is like being with a friend who has a will of their own. Explain why they say this.

2 Give examples of occasions when you have wanted to do or say a particular thing but haven't because something inside you has told you not to.

3 Religious people believe that this argument that sometimes goes on inside our heads between what we **want** to do and what we **ought** to do is often caused by God's will struggling with our will. What do you think?

4 Draw a picture or write a poem to illustrate a time when you have felt a kind of tension or disagreement going on inside yourself.

5 **Research work**
Religious people believe that particular Holy Books can give us a **greater** understanding of the **divine WILL** that struggles inside us. Read the following passages and explain what each of them says about **GOD'S WILL**. Also explain what God's will expects of us.

Psalm 19, verses 7–14
Psalm 36, verses 5–7
Isaiah chapter 6, verses 1–3
The Qur'an sura 4, verses 145–150
1 John chapter 4, verses 7–21
Mark chapter 12, verses 28–34